"Maggie Queeney's *settler* unites the tensions of domestic and wild, maker and object, homestead and horizon. Through constant refashioning of the sonnet, these poems stitch together like a quilt, alternating color and pattern, repurposing so nothing is wasted—no body song, no paper, no life. Every making is an offering. Within these pages, losses design our lives and the 'future dead are drawn from our body.' These poems startle, their quickening easy to feel beneath the page, Queeney's vein language bright and palpable."

—Traci Brimhall

"To live inside Maggie Queeney's *settler* is to be unraveled, bewitched, drawn back to the wonders of words and what we invent with them. In the words of Diane Seuss, 'There is something to be said for a boundary. There is also something to be said for an unbinding.' Through the poems' collective speaker, the reader is implied and thus invited to turn and return with Queeney, backward toward reverberations of grief and the genesis of language, forward toward birth and reinvention, 'The scream of the new voice / invading the old room.' These are holy sonnets for a new generation—Queeney reimagines form, challenging staid ideas of confinement, to gaze toward an edgy horizon, marveling at the sanctity of making, of language, of the human body, of pleasure and pain, of animal and earth."

—Jenny Molberg

T0083787

I

"Maggie Queeny's sonnet filled chapbook, *settler*, has a constrained, yet erudite and precise language with which to describe how settlers become their own occupiers in each quiet turn of thought. Told from the perspective of women who settle on the trail because of death and fever, they find themselves signing like their sheep who bleat against the harsh sky trying to survive. All is the physicality of the extremity of the natural world, reminding us Mother Nature is not a friendly hippie goddess of the 20th century, but one of the white bones and red blood of Mother Nature as femme fatale. Here ancestor is another name for someone who survived long enough, to say 'the future dead pulled from bodies' are what we leave to earth, a sacrifice and a scar. Here, poetry is also alive, pulled from a body of women's history, before we were liberated from the moon with hygiene and hospital births. The sculpted and beautiful, quiet language creates moments where chaos and order meet. *settler* inhabits a stunning and stern world, using well-crafted poems as a way to show us just how much progress we have made."

—Elizabeth Powell

settler

Maggie Queeney

TUPELO PRESS

CONTENTS

I.

II.

III.

I.

Female

We buttoned shut along our spines,
Padded skirts swinging bell-like
Along the knotted, the hewn plank walks
Above the mud, tentacle-strong, we float
In blooms and bandages, naked legs seen
Only by our husbands as they held
Our wax-white thighs on our wedding nights
Like two knives against that sharpening stone
Cutting out child after child. What we were for:
Breaking the animal down into parts
In the darkening house, the feeding lengths
Of wood to stove, parabolic needle
And thread to mend the tearing
Wearing our emptying clothes.

Sex

Our fathers and brothers rose unclothed,
White as bone against dark water, but still
We could not fathom what strange forms
Clapped under walls of wool pants, shirts blank

And unyielding as sheets. We halted
At the fur fastened to chest, to groin,
To pet or part. Even spring-learned,
Versed in the stock stuckw in paired,

Wailed mating we followed, melody
Or sermon revealing our own
First, blood-anointed uncleaving not found
In the hook and eye, pitchfork

And bale, hitch and coupling, heatless
Bleating, our cries recognized.

Crave

So much mean needing
Bottoms our stomachs, calluses
Hands, furs vision, keeps time
With the air wearing to bone.

Our bodies sing for salt, for fruit, the lard
Crackling the skillet bottom and shrouding
The lamb, snarl of rose petals, silver
Chains tracing breastbones, bathing

Infants slick as fish and know no world,
No immediate domain. No spangled
Night sky. Only the hand that stills
Us like livestock, the bellow that cores

Us, the spade blade that tunnels into
The high whine they take for singing.

Barren

Dry lighting, root-blighted, we
Render back into leg, arm
And waist, spine describing well
Without bottom. The month a measure-
Less ocean and sail-wrapped remains
Work miles of brine in a sliver—

Failed and flawed and begging,
We unkept, unkeeping, we take
Space, knead and bake, cut loam and bury
The blind seed, arrange rows long
And deep of jars' glare dim to the sun
Filtered under the door to reflect the aprons
White and luffing about our thighs, the faces
Shadow-middled, distended, light-edged.

Progeny

In unsteady firelight, we studied the arabesque clouds animated

In the plates of a yellowing page to find the girl born blue, her eyes

Two closed lines, impersonal as print or fossils, lasted not a month

Each, like a dream, haunt in half-recall; the river-swallowed

Boy, his small body never found after the flood returned

To earth, to the ocean where we imagined him floating

Asleep among bait fish and sharks, maroon-shrouded, lacelike

Seaweed, salt-glittering. He returns in nightmare, serpentine

Current wriggling from his mouth to baptize the floor. We caught

His mud-soft hands, offered buttermilk, lard-coated bread. Our loss

Part of a larger design, true, but the sky over us was always so blue

And empty and unbound, clouds shielding what heaven we knew of,

Darkened tally of grave mounds, the shadow so swift we were forced

To stare at the sun for what circled, dirt greening, year after year.

Birth

Blood anointed, this clawing inside-
Out, velvet purse inversion, slick
Life substance, vein language, scarlet
Inner lake running over. The woman attending
Thins the red with a darkening rag.
The children and men driven outside keep time
With our cries, the interval and pitch
Rising to howl, offering two ends

And our loss forked, doubled. From divergent
Thighs, hands pull at the crowning skull.
We clutch wood and sheets, to ward
Off what we will not later recollect—
The scream of the new voice
Invading the old room.

II.

Paper

Transmuted cotton; inner bark pounded;
Rags torn of clothing and boiled, that oiled
Chapped udders, shrouded the heirloom pendant;
Now bleached egg-white, white of milk molar;

Pounded thin and toothy. Elusive as shrews,
The soft coal hand slants into honed points
And loops soft as stitches, tight as a knit darkening
The page to each felted edge until the white

Turns negative, turns into the wasps' comb
Of cells of air, wood, spit, womb-mark
Of larvae that live as we would have lived:
To chew and by division multiply, cast our own

Size and shape; the familiar, unreadable lines
Of our illiterate hands, ruled face.

Hand

Her, always a her, hand on the dead-eyed
Slate at the front of the room, showing
How we should: the slanted lines
Like staves, lines climb and loop

Like the flags snaking the wind
Of lost battlefields. We traced
The strange tracks in ticcing stitches, her hand
As red, as rough and cracked

As our own, but her lines pulled true
As rows, letters certain as windows
We leaned into and through, echoing
What she sounded out:

Horizon-dark trees marking the line past
Where we would travel.

Sweet

Sugar leaves the tongue in a burn,
Sudden and haunting, scars the purse
Of the mouth clutched close, salved
In spit, head-hidden and empty.

Last season's apples, stewed, dried dull,
Yell, when we want what sings:
Christmas citrus rinds' porous, flame-
Licked sheen, mysterious as myrrh.

So little of what we have holds color,
Bites back. We, left, flex our jaws, trace
The sinuous weave of honey-heavy bees
To their aureate-gutted end

Among the other trunks bent into women
At the close of a day.

Cloth

We soften with our bodies the fistlets
Of primroses blurring into pastel burrs.
The stripes bleed, and netted plaid puddles
Into singular, unremarkable color.

Flowers shame us, petals curled into lashes,
Pared nail, joint cut, or feathers barbed
In hues without name, a shade *blue*
Only points to—

Mimic of rough walls, eyes on splintered lintels,
Cloaked in wood smoke, our parts separate
Along the seams, flattened into maps
Over the table. Unraveling threads expose

The unbroken wax of unsunned skin beneath
The pull and balance of warp and woof and weave.

Quilt

Salvage the blind cleaving, cuts

Of last years' dresses, felted denim,

Petticoats pleated fine as fungus

Unstrung and lined truer than horizon,

Than the cast spines of our knives,

Legs of our scissors, the black we stitch,

Hopeful as seeds, into ellipses bridging

An abandoned sleeve to chest pocket, waist

To sweat-darkened collar, we bind

Days to weeks and hours kaleidoscope

To cover the clothing-shorn resting forms

In revenant gestures, we piece the collective

Shroud, bridge our movements to cover

The ones left to touch and not remember

Mirror

Silver-meated, clouded, an unframed fragment
Kept like a sharp, ragged letter
Wrapped in cloth where a bladed flaw catches
Among the soft foxing of frost spots

The plane of our jaw visible, palm-sized
And shaped. Like a hand passing orbits—
Our face, part-lit as the moon, angle
Describing the unseen, hidden halves—

Unfathomable wholes of our own
Bottoming window, pocket or glance
Of or as the other, an optical stutter
Echoing the coronet of hair braided

By touch—ghost of our mothers bent
Over the faces of their men.

Pain

To the resting heart, boots pacing floorboard,
Stampeding herd amplified, a clock strikes,
Nails driven into green wood. Bolts
Of cloth torn and halved by hand. Lightning

Or snake track. Welling river, near-
Imperceptible, until whole houses sail
Like strange boats and stock swells, death-
Multiplied. Droning colonies itch,

Strike, and sting. Thorn digging, spade-
Turned, sickle-shorn. Flame-licked. Before
The boil, the plumes of steam. Cistern sweat.
Lake ice-dim and distant. The laboring,

Seam-split bellow. Whip flick or blade
Thrust, the fistlike heart, night incomplete.

III.

Homestead

We settled where stranded:

                          the hollow

Where the horse fell leg-by-leg
As if descending a staircase, snake-bit
And frothing; the purse puckered,
Stomach vacant; child fever-burnt bright
As a banked fire.

                    Now what holds us

Is the sweet water-swelled well;
Back taxes and small bills owed; hatchet-
Bites linking trunks into walls; crosses
Like stitches darkening the far field
And the bones we know glow
Milk-white even under a hide

Of dirt;

          the shape made of two bodies—one arm
Coiled round the other held down.

Animal

Unsouled, vibrating, we divide you
Into farmyard and dark wood, domestic
And wild, ancillary and enemy, industrious
And chaste, sly and designing.

Litters mewling blind disappear
Underwater, underground, into parts
Knife-cloven, between trees, or lengthen
Into bodies that offer to our bodies,

Our mouths and hands, milk and egg,
Leather and lard, meat and fur.
The wild, in woods, nest-curled, burrow-
Encircled, sharpen claw against dirt,

Fang against bone. Abed, in our own bodies,
Spine-divided, mirrored, we turn.

Longing

Afterimage without name: tentacles
Breaching sea-ceiling to clasp
Ship to white maw or the glow
Slow leaving of October, cheek

Of the first child born blue who we swore
We saw draw air. Lives quilted
Of news from alien continents, mating song
Of the unknown animal, the limbs of our men,

Made of our meals, then sent against winter,
Stone and stump, markets, while we bent
To tend the fires burning a flexing crown
In the heart of the house we would never

Wear. Another man. Another land. Form
Other than what was and not given.

Want

Who knew where had it been writ
Who to write what words we had learned
To name it gilt in the one book we owned and knew
The softening edges of the dark-anointed decades
Of pagings of what was read to us our eyes left to untangle
The letters of like fingers struck frost-dumb
Trying to strike the match and sound out the syllables
Of our quickening heartbeat

When it coiled in our stomachs wetted throat-back
Or burned our chest and neck a red we never saw
Outside our own blood did it take the snake
The fork-tongued form of the one we knew from engraved plate
Cloven-hooved furred horn the curve of our rising and setting
Stomach point tapered into the blank white meaning air

Horizon

World-rim, studded in distant buildings
Hunched under the insurmountable, constant
Streamer of weather. Harvest-blurred, leaf-tips scour
Cloud-ceiling, the ragged ring encircling, waves

Radiating from we, the source, widen as we
Rise, stand, and scan our hand-sheltered
Eyes along the memorized edges, the crops
Crosshatched into a constant, groaning blanket.

It follows, circumscribes, divides here
From not-here, ours and another's, sky
And ground—uncombed expanses we gave
Our name, cut and framed inside penning fence

Lines the claimed, the recognized, a where
Staring back into multiple beyond.

Loss

We would not count the liquid ones lost
In sudden blood curtaining our thighs.
We would not count the ones
Who outlived us, reached full growth,
Married and bore as we did,
Names multiplying, inked in the leaves
Where we too were named, numbered,
Entered. Only the ill, the broken bodies

That fevered and froze, bled and burned,
Resisted our arrangements for the final
Posed photograph. The clothes thin
For the next, and, in the dark, skirts
Pulled into burrows about our waists,
Future dead are drawn from our body.

Acknowledgments

"Progeny" appeared in *The Laurel Review*, Spring 2018

"Animal," "Paper," and "Hand," appeared in *Poetry Northwest*, Summer & Fall 2017

"Sex" and "Birth" appeared in *The Cincinnati Review*, Winter 2018

My appreciation for the Baltic Writing Residency Poetry Chapbook Contest for first creating a space for these poems in the world, with particular thanks to Shane McCrae for selecting this collection.

My deepest gratitude to everyone at Tupelo Press for giving *settler* a second life, especially Jeffrey Levine, Kristina Marie Darling, and Allison O'Keefe.

I want to thank the poets who wrote in community with me as I first drafted these poems: Holly Amos, Dolly Lemke, and Patrick Samuel. Cameron McGill, thank you for being a part of my pride, and for your support and encouragement.

This book is for Kate Garklavs.

Photo Credit: Cameron McGill

Maggie Queeney is a writer, visual artist, and educator. Recipient of the 2019 Stanley Kunitz Memorial Prize, The Ruth Stone Scholarship, and a 2019 Individual Artists Program Grant from the City of Chicago, her recent work can be found in *Hayden's Ferry Review, Colorado Review*, and *American Poetry Review*, among others. She reads and writes in Chicago, where she was born.

POETRY

"*settler* began haunting me while I was reading it for the first time, so that as soon as I finished it I wanted to read it over again. Maggie Queeney has captured so much human experience in such a small space—and in that small space, in even smaller spaces, sonnet by sonnet—and my admiration for the book, in parituclar for its taut clarity, from which its power to haunt derives, only increases each time I read it."

—Shane McCrae, author of *The Gilded Auction Block: Poems*

ISBN 9781946482631

51495 >

9 781946 482631

TUPELO PRESS
tupelopress.org